Glimmers of Laughter through Wistful Eyes

In twilight's glow, dreams softly tease,
Laughter lingers like a whispering breeze.
Through wistful eyes, we dance and sway,
Moments held close, never to stray.

Shadows of joy in memories bright,
Chasing the echoes of pure delight.
In laughter's embrace, we find our place,
Time halts in the warmth of a smile's grace.

Chasing Rainbows After the Rain

In the aftermath of the stormy night,
Colors bloom where shadows take flight.
Chasing rainbows, a path to the sky,
Hope's gentle whisper, soaring high.

With every drop, the earth finds its song,
A melody sweet, where we all belong.
Hand in hand, through puddles we run,
Chasing the light, embracing the fun.

Playful Echoes of Heartfelt Longing

In secret corners where memories dwell,
Echoes of laughter cast a magical spell.
Heartfelt whispers in the cool night air,
Longing sways gently, a spirited flare.

With each fleeting moment, we pause and sigh,
The bittersweet taste of a lullaby.
Playful shadows around us intertwine,
A dance of the heart, your rhythm is mine.

Giggling Under the Weight of Woe

Beneath the weight of burdens we bear,
Giggling softly, a spark in our stare.
In the heaviness, laughter finds light,
A balm for the soul, igniting the fright.

With each tender chuckle, we ease the pain,
In the smallest joys, we flourish again.
Underneath clouds, we play and we bloom,
Giggling together, dispelling the gloom.

Melodies of Mirth in Melancholy

In shadows deep, a soft note plays,
Whispers of joy in gloomy haze.
Laughter dances, though tears may fall,
Melodies echo, embracing all.

A symphony of heart and woe,
Finding warmth in winter's glow.
Every heartbeat, a tune so sweet,
In sorrow's arms, our spirits meet.

Sunshine Sprinkled on Cloudy Days

Golden rays break through the gray,
Hope sprouts in the most unlikely way.
Clouds may gather, shadows loom,
Yet light persists, dispelling gloom.

A gentle breeze, the flowers sway,
Beauty blossoms in disarray.
Through every storm, the sun will shine,
In every heart, a light divine.

Embracing the Beauty of Broken Joy

Fragments glimmer, soft and bright,
Scattered pieces hold sheer delight.
In every crack, a new rebirth,
Finding strength in what it's worth.

Shattered dreams, yet still we stand,
Holding tight to love's warm hand.
In brokenness, we find our way,
Embracing life day by day.

The Sweetness of Bitter Revelations

Truth unveiled through a bitter tear,
Lessons learned can draw us near.
In shadows cast, a light is found,
Sweetness blooms from pain unbound.

Every scar tells tales of plight,
Hidden glory in darkest night.
Bitter roots give rise to grace,
Sweet revelations we embrace.

Whispers of Joyful Sorrow

In twilight's glow, soft echoes sigh,
Where laughter dances, but tears may lie.
A bittersweet song, the heart's duet,
In every joy, a hint of regret.

The sun can shine through a curtain of gray,
Binding the heart in a tender ballet.
With every heartbeat, a story unfolds,
Of joyful sorrow, the truth it holds.

Ribbons of Smiles in the Rain

Beneath grey clouds, the world feels bright,
As raindrops fall, they kiss the night.
Splashing colors that dance and twirl,
In puddles, joy begins to unfurl.

With ribbons of smiles, we splash and play,
Letting the rain wash our cares away.
Laughter echoes through the droplets' song,
In every storm, we find where we belong.

Melancholy's Sweet Embrace

In shadows deep, where memories dwell,
Melancholy whispers a soothing spell.
A gentle caress, a soft lullaby,
Holding our hearts in its tender sigh.

The silver lining of heartache's touch,
Reminds us that pain can teach us so much.
In the warmth of sorrow, we come to find,
A beauty in trials that frees the mind.

Glistening Grins Through the Shadows

In darkened woods where silence creeps,
A glimmer shines and softly leaps.
Glistening grins break through the night,
Chasing away the remnants of fright.

With every smile that lights the way,
Hopeful hearts find paths to stay.
Through shadows cast, love intertwines,
In glistening moments, the spirit shines.

Dancing in the Downpour

Rain falls soft, a gentle kiss,
Feet tap light in puddles' bliss.
Twirl and swirl, the heart takes flight,
In this dance, the world feels right.

Splashing colors, shoes all wet,
Laughter echoes, no regret.
Nature's rhythm, wild and free,
In the storm, we learn to be.

Clouds above, a curtain drawn,
In the chaos, we are reborn.
Every drip, a heartbeat's song,
Together we will dance along.

Heartstrings Sing in Shade

In the cool beneath the trees,
Whispers float upon the breeze.
Hearts entwined in silken light,
In this shade, our dreams take flight.

Gentle laughter fills the air,
Moments linger, sweet and rare.
Hands held close, a silent vow,
Here and now, it's ours somehow.

Songs of love, in soft retreat,
Every melody bittersweet.
Underneath this canopy,
Our heartstrings play in harmony.

Sweet Sobs of Serenity

Tears like rain fall from the heart,
In their depth, we find our art.
Softly flowing, quiet grace,
In each sob, we find our place.

Whispers of a silent night,
Moonbeams cast a soothing light.
With each sigh, the spirit mends,
Soft resolve, as pain transcends.

In the stillness, solace found,
Sweet embraces all around.
Healing blooms with every cry,
In the tears, our spirits fly.

Smiling Through the Storm

Lightning flashes, thunder roars,
Yet the heart opens its doors.
Winds may howl, but we stand tall,
In the storm, we'll never fall.

Raindrops tap a joyful tune,
Dancing shadows with the moon.
Through the chaos, hope remains,
In the struggle, love sustains.

Brighter days will greet the dawn,
With each challenge, we move on.
Though tempests rage, we will smile,
Side by side, we'll go each mile.

The Juxtaposition of Joy and Regret

In laughter's light, shadows arise,
Joy dances bright, but sorrow sighs.
Memories tethered, moments held tight,
The heart in conflict, day and night.

Echoes of laughter, bittersweet sound,
In every triumph, regrets abound.
Joy's fleeting grasp, like sand in hand,
A delicate balance we strive to understand.

Giggles in the Gloom

In darkness thick, a giggle blooms,
A flicker of light in shadowed rooms.
Whispers of mirth, break through despair,
A soft reminder that joy is rare.

Under the weight of a heavy shroud,
Laughter persists, forging a crowd.
Through heavy clouds, a silver line,
Giggles in gloom, a sweet design.

Midnight Murmurs of Mirth

As stars awaken, secrets unfold,
Mirth rides the night, fiery and bold.
Beneath the moon's soft, silvery glow,
Midnight breathes joy, in whispers low.

Laughter echoes, a sweet serenade,
In the shadowed corners where memories played.
Every chuckle, a gentle friend,
In the still of night, where dreams transcend.

Wistful Whispers in the Wind

A breeze carries tales, both old and new,
Wistful whispers, memories ensue.
In the rustling leaves, stories unfold,
Gentle reminders of life's warmth and cold.

Through winding paths, the heart must roam,
Whispers in the wind, calling us home.
Each breath a tribute, each sigh a thread,
Woven in time, where all has been said.

The Palette of Pain and Pleasure

In shadows cast by twilight glow,
Brush strokes reveal the undertow.
Pain dances with pleasure's sweet embrace,
A canvas marked by time and grace.

Colors swirl in a tempest's wake,
Every heartbeat, a choice to make.
Sorrow sings in vibrant hues,
While joy blooms with every muse.

Ripples of Rapture and Regret

Gentle waves lap the sandy shore,
Echoes of laughter, whispers of lore.
Moments fleeting, a shimmering sight,
In twilight's glow, wrongs feel right.

Rapture twinkles like stars above,
Regret lingers, yet hides in love.
Each splash carries a tale unrevealed,
In ocean's heart, secrets concealed.

A Carnival of Contrasts

Under the tent, joy meets despair,
A juggler's dance, a tightrope's air.
Bright balloons against a stormy sky,
Laughter echoes, then a silent cry.

Colors clash in a vivid display,
Mirrored reflections lead hearts astray.
Amidst the chaos, we find our place,
In every contrast, a fleeting grace.

Serenade of Smiles and Sighs

Beneath the moon, soft whispers flow,
A serenade, where feelings grow.
Smiles linger in the cool night air,
While sighs of longing drift everywhere.

In this dance of joy and pain,
Hearts together, yet bound by chain.
In each note, a story unfolds,
A tapestry woven with dreams and holds.

Paintbrushes of Grief and Glee

In shadows deep where colors blend,
A tearful brush does softly send,
Stroke of sorrow, stroke of cheer,
On canvas wide, both far and near.

The hues of pain, a vibrant red,
Joy's golden rays, though often spread,
Each layer tells a tale untold,
Of bittersweet lives, both brave and bold.

With every sweep, emotions burst,
From heart's whisper to vocal thirst,
Painted skies of joy and strife,
A masterpiece reflects our life.

In every brush, a story lies,
In laughter's echo, in sorrow's cries,
Together they dance in twilight's light,
Painting our days, both dark and bright.

The Kinship of Dismal Delight

In shadows cast by fleeting dreams,
Where laughter hides, or so it seems,
The joy of grief, a tangled thread,
In silent halls where silence led.

A bittersweet embrace unfolds,
In whispered truths, the heart beholds,
The kinship found in tear-streaked smiles,
In every woe, the joy beguiles.

Through starlit nights, and raining skies,
A mournful song still gently flies,
For in the depths of dark despair,
A flicker, faint, of hope shines rare.

Dismal delight, both cruel and kind,
In shadows bright, true joys we find,
Together they dwell, a shared refrain,
In life's embrace, both love and pain.

Laughter that Lingers like a Moonlit Memory

In whispers soft beneath the night,
Where laughter dances, pure delight,
Like moonbeams grazing sleepy streams,
It lingers sweet in tender dreams.

Each chuckle shared a spark ignites,
In quiet corners of starry nights,
The echoes trail like silver threads,
Binding hearts where joy still spreads.

Though time may drift like clouds above,
Those fleeting moments filled with love,
Become the stars that guide our way,
In every night, in every day.

So let us cherish, hold them tight,
These memories wrapped in soft moonlight,
For laughter lives where we once played,
In echoes sweet, our hearts arrayed.

Echoing Happiness in Heartbreak

In heart's embrace, the sorrow sings,
Yet echoes of joy spread gentle wings,
For every tear that falls anew,
A thread of laughter weaves right through.

The dance of pain, a solemn tune,
Creates a space for joy to bloom,
In heartbreak's grip, there lies a spark,
To light the way through endless dark.

In every ache, a lesson learned,
The fire of hope, forever burned,
With every sigh, a smile breaks free,
Echoing through, life's harmony.

So let the heart in fragments dwell,
For within the cracks, there's magic swell,
In joy's soft whisper, find your way,
Through every night, into the day.

Serenade of Sorrowful Smiles

In the garden where shadows dwell,
Whispers of laughter, a distant bell.
Petals fall like tears on the ground,
Echoes of joy that can no longer be found.

Underneath the moon's pale light,
A heart that aches in the still of night.
Yet amidst the sorrow, a fragile thread,
We weave our dreams from words unsaid.

Faded memories dance in the air,
Haunting the silence, a ghostly stare.
Yet smiles emerge, through pain they break,
A serenade of the love we forsake.

In the twilight, we find our song,
Sorrowful smiles where we once belonged.
Let the music play, bittersweet and true,
For in our hearts, there's a melody of you.

Bubbles of Bliss Amidst the Blues

Bubbles rising in the evening sway,
Floating gently, they chase the gray.
Colorful whispers fill the air,
Light as laughter, beyond despair.

In the laughter, find a twinkling shade,
Moments of joy in the dreams we made.
Crisp and clear, a delicate sigh,
Bubbles of bliss that refuse to die.

Drifting softly on a warm breeze,
Holding the spark of forgotten ease.
In the depths of night, they gleam and glow,
A promise of sunshine, a gentle flow.

Though blues might linger, we rise above,
Bubbles of happiness wrapped in love.
Each burst a reminder that life can sing,
Amidst the dark, let our spirits take wing.

When Joy Weeps Softly

In the quiet corners of the heart,
Joy weeps softly, a poignant art.
Tears of laughter, bittersweet grace,
In a dance of shadows, we find our place.

Colored rainbows in a glass of dew,
Glimmers of hope piercing through the blue.
Unraveling tales of love and loss,
When joy weeps softly, we bear the cross.

Each drop a memory, a story untold,
Whispering secrets as the night grows old.
Through every sigh, in the still of time,
Joy softly weeps, a delicate rhyme.

Yet in this sorrow, a strength resides,
Holding us close, like the ebbing tides.
When joy weeps softly, we learn to heal,
Embracing the pain, we begin to feel.

Smiling in the Storm's Embrace

When thunder rolls and the skies turn gray,
We find our courage, come what may.
Smiling truths in the tempest's roar,
Holding the warmth of what we adore.

Through wind's wild dance, we stand our ground,
Hearts intertwined, a love profound.
Raindrops like jewels touch our skin,
In the storm's embrace, we let love in.

Each flash of lightning, a moment bright,
Guiding our steps through the darkest night.
With smiles as shields, we face the fray,
In the storm's embrace, we'll find our way.

So let the clouds gather, we won't despair,
For love is the compass, forever our care.
In every storm, when chaos reigns,
We'll smile together, through joys and pains.

The Essence of Elegy and Exuberance

In shadows deep, the whispers sway,
A dance of grief, yet hope holds sway.
Through tears we learn, through pain we grow,
The heart can ache, but love will flow.

In twilight's glow, we find our peace,
Memories bloom, and sorrows cease.
Each loss a gem, each tear a light,
A tapestry woven, dark and bright.

With hands raised high, we celebrate,
The essence living in our fate.
Through elegy, we rise anew,
In every heart, a spark breaks through.

A Carnival of Emotions

Beneath the tents of vibrant cheer,
A whirlwind of feelings draws us near.
Joyful laughter, a bittersweet song,
In this carnival, we all belong.

With painted faces and masks of light,
We dance through darkness, embrace the night.
Each smile a ray, each tear a tide,
In this grand parade, we take each stride.

A flicker of fear, a flash of delight,
In every heartbeat, the ups and downs ignite.
Emotions collide, like colors so bold,
A tapestry of stories yet untold.

Laughter in the Labyrinth of Loss

In winding paths where shadows loom,
Laughter echoes, dispelling gloom.
Each twist and turn, a story told,
A heart that breaks, yet learns to hold.

Beneath the grief, a spark remains,
In laughter's chase, we heal the pains.
Through every corner, we seek the light,
In a labyrinth built of fragile night.

With every chuckle, we find our way,
Embracing sorrow, come what may.
For in the depths of what we miss,
Laughter is found, a cherished bliss.

The Symphony of Sighs and Smiles

In twilight realms where silence sings,
A symphony of subtle things.
Sighs weave through, like threads of gold,
While smiles bloom bright, a tale unfolds.

With every note, a memory played,
In joy and sorrow, we are arrayed.
The heartstrings strum with gentle grace,
A dance of emotions in sacred space.

Through whispered dreams, the chords entwine,
In every sigh, a story divine.
Together we rise, through every storm,
In this symphony, our spirits warm.

Harmonizing Hurt and Happiness

In shadows deep, where sorrows lie,
A flicker of light, a gentle sigh.
Through tangled paths, we find our way,
In pain's embrace, we learn to stay.

The heart can ache, but also sing,
Tears can spark the joy they bring.
A dance of emotions, intertwined,
In every hurt, a gift we find.

The laughter echoes in the night,
Where memories glow, soft and bright.
Embracing both, we grow and mend,
In hurt and happiness, we blend.

A symphony of what we feel,
With every wound, the heart can heal.
So let us cherish, hand in hand,
In life's sweet chaos, we shall stand.

Moments like Raindrops

Moments fall like raindrops clear,
Each one whispers, drawing near.
They splash on hearts, a gentle tune,
In fleeting echoes, we are strewn.

A soft embrace, a fleeting glance,
In every drop, we find a chance.
To dance beneath the silver skies,
And find the beauty in the cries.

Some fade away, some linger near,
Each precious second, crystal clear.
In storms of life, we learn to trust,
To gather moments, rise from dust.

Like raindrops falling on the earth,
They spark the seeds of love and mirth.
In every storm, there's light to see,
Moments like raindrops, wild and free.

The Bright Side of Brokenness

From shattered dreams, new dreams arise,
In brokenness, we find the skies.
A kaleidoscope of colors bright,
In every fracture, hidden light.

Though pieces scatter, hearts can mend,
A sacred journey, we transcend.
For in the cracks, we learn to grow,
And let our true selves bravely show.

With every tear, a lesson learned,
In wrestling loss, our souls are turned.
The bright side shines through darkest nights,
In brokenness, we find our fights.

So let the shards reflect our grace,
A tapestry, life's sweet embrace.
The bright side waits for us to see,
In brokenness, we are set free.

Glistening Moments of Melancholy

In twilight's glow, the shadows dance,
Glistening moments, lost in trance.
Melancholy whispers soft and low,
In every sigh, a tale we know.

The heart feels heavy, yet it glows,
In quiet depths, that beauty flows.
A teardrop shines like morning dew,
In somber hues, a world anew.

Each lingering thought holds weight and grace,
In the stillness, we find our place.
Embracing all that feels so real,
In moments lost, our spirits heal.

So let us cherish what we feel,
The glistening tales that time will seal.
In melancholy, we find the spark,
A gentle glow within the dark.

Splashes of Sunshine and Sadness

Golden rays kiss the ground,
Whispers of joy and sorrow,
In each smile, a tear is found,
Chasing dreams we cannot borrow.

Laughter dances on the breeze,
While shadows linger near,
Moments soft as autumn leaves,
Intwined with threads of fear.

Yet in the warmth of daylight's grace,
Hope flickers like a flame,
Creating beauty in this space,
Where sunshine meets the pain.

Bound in nature's tender arms,
We find a bittersweet refrain,
In every joy, a quiet charm,
In splashes of sunshine and sadness' gain.

Melancholic Merriment

Smiling faces hide the ache,
In the revelry, we dwell,
Beneath the laughter, hearts might break,
A sorrow deep we know too well.

Jesters dance, the music swells,
Joyful strains mask disbelief,
In merry tales, a truth compels,
To seek solace in our grief.

The jingle of the bells can sound,
With echoes of what's lost,
Melancholy wraps around,
Yet merriment pays the cost.

In fleeting joy, we lose and gain,
A paradox we come to face,
Dance through the laughter, through the pain,
In this melancholic space.

Hues of Laughter and Longing

Colors blend in twilight's glow,
Echoes of laughter swirl and play,
Yet in the bright, a hint of woe,
Longing shadows weight the day.

Painted skies with hues of red,
Vibrant tales of joy to tell,
But underneath the dreams we've fed,
Is a yearning we know well.

Every chuckle has its edge,
Cascading ripples carry dreams,
In every smile, we make a pledge,
To navigate our silent screams.

With every hue, a truth unfolds,
In laughter's light, we seek our peace,
Though longing whispers may be bold,
In shades of joy, we find release.

Serenades for Sunny Shadows

Soft melodies in the air,
Sung by shadows on the ground,
Each note whispers a gentle prayer,
For moments lost but still abound.

Beneath the sun, where shadows play,
A serenade for hearts concealed,
Joy in sorrow, night in day,
In silence, wounds are revealed.

Swaying branches, heartfelt tunes,
In dancing light, we find our way,
Through the laughter and by the moons,
The shadows whisper what we say.

In every note, a hidden song,
Of love, of loss, a tender cast,
For in the sun, where we belong,
Serenades for shadows last.

Whispers of Happiness and Heartache

In shadows dance the sweet refrain,
A melody of joy and pain.
Each laughter hides a silent tear,
Where love once bloomed, now lingers fear.

A whispered word, a fleeting glance,
A moment that ignites romance.
Yet in the light, the shadows creep,
For hearts that love must often weep.

The sun can rise and set again,
Each heartbeat leads to joy or pain.
In every smile, a hint of sorrow,
But hope can guide us to tomorrow.

So dance within this fragile space,
Embrace the smiles, the tears we trace.
For happiness and heartache dwell,
Together in a magic spell.

Liquid Sunshine

Golden drops like morning dew,
Fill the sky with shades of blue.
Liquid sunshine, warm and bright,
Painting dreams in soft daylight.

Feel the warmth upon your skin,
A gentle touch that draws you in.
Every ray a soft caress,
In nature's arms, we find our rest.

Rivers flow with laughter loud,
As sunbeams dance in silver cloud.
Nature sings her shimm'ring song,
In harmony, we all belong.

So raise your cup to skies so blue,
To liquid sunshine, fresh and true.
In every droplet, joy we find,
A tender link, no ties that bind.

The Paradox of Grief and Glee

In laughter's echo, sorrow hides,
A playful game where heart abides.
Through joy we taste the hint of pain,
In sunshine's grasp, we feel the rain.

Moments fleeting, bright and dark,
Each memory leaves a tender mark.
For every smile, a shadow looms,
A dance of joy amidst the glooms.

Yet in the contrast, we find light,
Two sides of life, both bold and bright.
Grief and glee, a delicate thread,
In woven tales, our spirits wed.

So honor both, let feelings blend,
In paradox, we shall transcend.
For through the tears, the laughter flows,
A tapestry that life bestows.

Melodies of Mirthful Memory

In twilight glow, the memories sing,
With echoing laughter, warmth they bring.
Each note, a whisper of the past,
A fleeting moment, meant to last.

The sweet refrain of days gone by,
Painted in hues of the azure sky.
In wisps of joy and shades of grace,
We find a smile on every face.

When melodies of mirth arise,
They dance and twirl before our eyes.
In every heartbeat, stories weave,
A tapestry we dare believe.

So let us celebrate the sound,
Of joyful moments, love unbound.
In memory, there's magic true,
A melody that sings of you.

Radiant Rivulets of Reminiscence

In the twilight glow of fading days,
Memories dance in gentle sways.
Soft whispers brush the evening air,
Time weaves tales beyond compare.

Each droplet glimmers, a story told,
Of laughter shared and dreams of old.
Reflecting light that warms the heart,
In tranquil streams, we find our art.

Through winding paths of past delight,
We wander back into the night.
These rivulets of joy and pain,
Flow timelessly, yet feel the same.

As shadows stretch and moments fade,
In silent thoughts, memories wade.
Their radiant glow will ever stay,
A beacon bright to light the way.

Laughter Beneath the Clouds

Beneath the clouds, where dreams collide,
Laughter lingers, hearts open wide.
A symphony of joy and cheer,
With every giggle, we draw near.

The raindrops fall, a rhythmic beat,
Yet in the storm, our spirits meet.
We twirl and dance, no care in sight,
For in this moment, souls take flight.

Through gray skies brightened by our glee,
We find the light, we choose to be.
In puddles deep, we splash and play,
It's laughter's warmth that leads the way.

So let the clouds roll in with grace,
For joy will always find its place.
With laughter's ring, we hold the loud,
Our joy resounds beneath the cloud.

The Taste of Bittersweet Echoes

In twilight's hush, remnants of sighs,
Bittersweet echoes, where memory lies.
Each taste a blend of joy and pain,
In every drop, love's bitters reign.

We linger long on moments gone,
While shadows sing their dusky song.
The heart remembers what time won't break,
In echoes soft, the past we take.

A touch of bitters on the tongue,
Reminds us well of songs once sung.
Through happiness and sorrow's kiss,
We find a depth in every bliss.

In every note, a heart does yearn,
For in the echo, we discern.
The sweetness found in sorrow's trace,
Is where we find our saving grace.

Joyful Echoes of Silent Cries

In quiet moments, hearts align,
Joyful echoes, both yours and mine.
In silent cries, our truths are told,
Through laughter's light, we break the cold.

Hidden beneath a smiling face,
Are tales of love, a warm embrace.
For every tear that fell like rain,
A joyful echo shall remain.

Though silence wraps the weary night,
We find in shadows, hints of light.
In whispered hopes and dreams reside,
A tapestry where feelings hide.

So let the echoes softly chime,
In every heart, a song in rhyme.
With every breath, we rise anew,
Joyful echoes, strong and true.

Whispered Secrets of the Heart

In the quiet of the night, we sigh,
Soft murmurs, a gentle goodbye.
Our dreams weave tales in the dark,
Holding each other, we leave a mark.

Voices linger, secrets unfold,
Stories of love, tender and bold.
Each wish whispered on a breeze,
Carried away with such ease.

Words unspoken, yet understood,
In this silence, we find our good.
Hearts entwined, a sacred trust,
Bound together, in hope we must.

In the dawn's light, truths emerge,
With every heartbeat, feelings surge.
Holding tight to what we share,
In whispered secrets, we lay bare.

Shadows that Sparkle

Beneath the stars, a dance begins,
Shadows waltz, where light thins.
Glimmers peek through the night's embrace,
A shimmering veil, a hidden place.

With every turn, the night ignites,
Dreams awaken, reaching new heights.
In the darkness, our hearts take flight,
Finding magic in soft starlight.

Laughter echoes, the moon listens,
Radiant twinkles where hope glistens.
Whispers flow in the cool night air,
Painting memories, bold and rare.

Together we chase the fleeting gleam,
In shadows that sparkle, we dare to dream.
Hand in hand, through the midnight haze,
Creating our light, in a thousand ways.

Chasing the Confetti of Tears

Raindrops fall like confetti bright,
Coloring the world in pure delight.
Each tear carries a story, a song,
In the dance of sorrow, we find where we belong.

A cascade of moments, joyful yet sad,
Chasing memories, both good and bad.
In the aftermath of a stormy tear,
We gather the fragments, hold them near.

Laughter and cries, they intertwine,
Every emotion, a precious line.
With every drop, we learn to forgive,
Finding solace in the way we live.

Chasing the confetti that slips from our eyes,
We learn to see through the clouded skies.
In the chaos, beauty does appear,
In every tear, there's a spark of cheer.

Reflections in a Pool of Delights

Glimmers of joy in waters deep,
Mirrored wishes, secrets we keep.
Ripples dance with every sigh,
In the stillness, time slips by.

Beneath the surface, dreams unfold,
Stories waiting, yet untold.
In the depths, we find our light,
Guided by stars in the quiet night.

Each reflection tells a tale,
Of heartbeats, hopes, and a gentle sail.
Together we weave through shadows and glare,
In this pool of delights, we dare to care.

Floating softly on waves of fate,
Moments gathered, nothing late.
In the embrace of tranquil dives,
We find the magic that truly thrives.

A Serenade of Smiling Sobs

In a whisper of tears, the heart does sing,
Melodies rise where the shadows cling.
With each sob, a laughter born anew,
In the silence, a symphony breaks through.

Beneath the moon's glow, the night unfolds,
Stories of heartaches that life beholds.
Dancing with echoes of joy and pain,
A serenade woven through heart's refrain.

Through the cracks, the light gently spills,
Painting the soul with colorful thrills.
Smiling hugs hidden in every cry,
A tune of hope that never says die.

So let the tears fall, like soft summer rain,
Each droplet cherished, never in vain.
For in the sobs, a truth we find,
A serenade of joy intertwined.

Laughter as a Shield Against the Shadows.

In the darkest alley, laughter rings loud,
A beacon of hope, standing so proud.
With every chuckle, the shadows retreat,
Light in our hearts, making us complete.

Jokes like arrows, piercing the gloom,
Chasing away what dares to assume.
Guarding our spirits with joyous sound,
In laughter's embrace, we are unbound.

A shield of mirth against sorrow's might,
Transforming our fears into pure delight.
With friends gathered close, the worries depart,
Laughter's sweet rhythm, a balm for the heart.

So let us chuckle as the world sways,
In our laughter, the shadows ablaze.
For joy is the armor we wear each day,
A shield against shadows that come out to play.

Echoes of Joyful Sorrow

In the realm where joy and sorrow dance,
Echoes of laughter, each tear, a chance.
Together they weave a tapestry bright,
Building a bridge from darkness to light.

Moments of bliss wrapped in soft despair,
Every whisper carries the weight of care.
Yet in the sorrow, the beauty we find,
Echoes of joy, gently intertwined.

So lift up your voice in the bittersweet twine,
Celebrate the moments that solemnly shine.
For in every heartbeat, both shadow and light,
Echoes of joy bring the stars into sight.

A symphony played on the strings of the soul,
Merging the parts to create a whole.
In joyful sorrow, the depths we explore,
The echoes remind us there's always more.

Glistening Smiles in the Rain

In the drumming rain, smiles start to glisten,
Whispers of joy that beg us to listen.
Puddles reflect the laughter we share,
Dancing together, without a care.

Each raindrop's kiss paints colors anew,
A canvas of memories, vibrant and true.
In rain's gentle lullaby, spirits take flight,
Glistening smiles set the world alight.

Embracing the storm with hearts open wide,
Finding the magic where dreams coincide.
Letting the rain wash the worries away,
Glistening smiles brighten the gray.

So let the clouds gather, let the rivers flow,
For smiles in the rain help our spirits grow.
With laughter like thunder, joy will remain,
Forever we shine, even in the rain.

Echoes of Glee and Grief

In the garden where shadows play,
Laughter lingers, then fades away.
Joy entwined with sorrow's sigh,
Memories dance, as moments fly.

Whispers of love, both near and far,
Echo through nights like a distant star.
Tears that shimmer in morning light,
Remind us of what feels so right.

Bright smiles twinkle through the haze,
A fleeting glimpse of a sunlit phase.
Yet in the heart, the ache will stay,
Glee and grief in a fragile ballet.

Still we find strength in each refrain,
Holding close both joy and pain.
Life's symphony plays on and on,
In every dusk, we cherish dawn.

Sweetness Found in Brokenness

Amidst the cracks, new blooms arise,
Through brokenness, hope never dies.
Petals soft in the morning dew,
Whisper tales of the past we knew.

Tender scars, like silver threads,
Weaving stories of joys and dreads.
Each fragment tells of battles fought,
In the silence, sweet lessons taught.

From weary roots, the branches spread,
Stronger now, from tears we've shed.
Through the storms, we learn to soar,
Sweetness born from struggles we bore.

Embrace the flaws, let color shine,
In brokenness, we find design.
Life stitches dreams with threads of grace,
In every heart, love finds its place.

Laughter's Veil Over Mourning

In laughter's arms, the sorrow hides,
Dancing softly where heartache bides.
Through the cracks, a chuckle breaks,
Light embraces, though the silence aches.

Grief wears a mask, a playful guise,
While joy flickers in tired eyes.
Moments shared, a bittersweet charm,
We gather close, finding warmth in the calm.

Echoes of laughter fill the air,
A reminder that love is always there.
As we gather, both heavy and light,
Together we stand, embracing the night.

With every giggle, healing begins,
In sorrow's mist, new hope spins.
Laughter's veil wraps tight and safe,
In memories shared, we find our grace.

Dancing with Delightful Heartache

In twilight's glow, emotions swell,
Dancing hearts, we cast our spell.
Every beat, a story told,
In the rhythm, both soft and bold.

Twisting shadows lead the way,
Through the fragments of yesterday.
Each step whispers a lingering sigh,
In the dance of dreams, we learn to fly.

With graceful moves, our hearts embrace,
The joy of love and the sorrow we face.
Every twirl, a memory spun,
In heartache's grip, we find our fun.

Delight in the ache, we learn to sway,
In every loss, find lightness to play.
So let us dance, come what may,
In the joyful pain, we find our way.

The Taste of Joyful Regrets

Memories linger like sweet perfume,
Whispers of laughter in a quiet room.
Moments we savored, now bittersweet,
A dance with time, on weary feet.

We cherish the echoes of dreams once bright,
Fleeting as shadows fading from sight.
Yet in our hearts, a warmth remains,
An ache that comforts, a love that sustains.

Time may rewrite the stories we tell,
Yet in our hearts, all is well.
For every parting, there's a hello,
In joyful regrets, our spirits grow.

So we raise a glass to the paths we chose,
Sipping on memories like wind-blown prose.
With every sigh, a smile will ignite,
The taste of joyful regrets feels just right.

Smiles Flecked with Grief

Amidst the laughter, shadows creep,
Smiles concealing what we keep.
In joy's embrace, we sometimes hide,
The tender ache that swells inside.

For every grin, a tear may trail,
In the beauty, we feel the frail.
Woven together, joy and woe,
Each fleeting moment, ebb and flow.

We wear our brightness like a star,
Yet know that grief is never far.
In every chuckle, a sigh persists,
A testament to the love we miss.

So let us dance through joy and pain,
Finding balance in the rain.
For smiles flecked with grief still shine,
A portrait of love, forever divine.

The Sweetness of Lost Laughter

In a quiet room where echoes stay,
Laughter resounds from a brighter day.
Though time has taken its merry toll,
The sweetness lingers, filling our soul.

We gather the moments like fallen leaves,
In the heart's garden, where memory weaves.
With every chuckle, a story unfurls,
The warmth of laughter, a world of pearls.

Yet with each smile, a longing grows,
For laughter shared with those we chose.
In whispers of joy, their voices play,
A symphony of the past in gentle sway.

And so we cherish each sound, each tune,
The sweetness of lost laughter a soft monsoon.
For in our hearts where echoes reside,
The joy of remembering will always abide.

Gentle Rain on a Radiant Day

Drops of joy kiss the sunlit ground,
A soothing rhythm, a calming sound.
Gentle rain falls where petals sway,
Nurturing life in a radiant way.

Each droplet dances in sun's warm light,
Painting the world in colors bright.
A soft embrace that nature shares,
Whispers of love in the fragrant airs.

As leaves shimmer under the gray,
We find peace in moments that play.
For even in storms, there lies delight,
Gentle rain brings forth new sight.

So let us walk through this tender scene,
Where joy and sorrow blend in between.
In gentle rain on a radiant day,
We find our hearts in the balance sway.

The Harmonious Collision of Heartache and Happiness

In shadows cast by fleeting dreams,
Joy dances on the edge of pain,
A bittersweet symphony it seems,
Where laughter mingles with disdain.

Moments cherished, moments lost,
Life's tapestry, a tangled thread,
Emotions shift, like waves they toss,
In heart's embrace, we move ahead.

Tender whispers in the night,
Echoes of a love once bright,
Through the heartache, light does flow,
Revealing strength we often know.

Yet in this clash of dark and light,
A truce is found, a gentle sight,
For in our hearts, both dwell as one,
A melody of night and sun.

Sweet Lamentations in Laughter's Glow

Beneath the smiles, a sorrow lies,
With every chuckle, tears can rise,
The joy we seek, the ache we hide,
In laughter's glow, we coincide.

Moments where the world feels right,
Yet shadows linger out of sight,
In every giggle, a hint of pain,
Sweet lamentations weave the grain.

Voices rising, hearts entwined,
Celebrating what we're yet to find,
In humor's grasp, a tender grace,
Finding solace in this space.

Through fragile laughs, we carry on,
In the stillness, a hopeful dawn,
For every ache that marks our way,
Laughter blooms, come what may.

Jests Wrapped in Gentle Grief

A quiet jest in the quiet morn,
Wrapped in layers of sorrow's thread,
A gentle smile for hearts that mourn,
The fragile lines of joy we spread.

Through playful banter, comfort glows,
Like sunlight peeking through the trees,
In every joke, a heart still grows,
In laughter's hands, the soul finds ease.

With each shared laugh, the past does fade,
Yet echoes linger in the breeze,
In jest, we find the love we've made,
A blend of grief that softly sees.

In tender moments, we unite,
Carrying both darkness and light,
For life, it seems, holds space for both,
In grief, a jest; in jest, our oath.

The Lightness of Heavy Hearts

Heavy hearts can still dance light,
In twilight's glow, we chase the night,
With burdens worn like precious lace,
We twirl in grief, find our own space.

The weight we bear is not in vain,
Each tear we shed, a drop of rain,
Together, we create a stream,
A river formed from every dream.

In laughter shared, our spirits soar,
Though shadows loom, we seek for more,
In joyous moments, sting of ache,
The lightness felt, for love's own sake.

Through trials faced, we lift the veil,
In every whisper, every tale,
The heavy hearts that beat in time,
Can find the strength in every rhyme.

A Tapestry of Grief and Giggles

In twilight's glow, a laughter weaves,
Through tears that fall like autumn leaves.
A bittersweet song plays in the air,
With echoes of joy and whispers of care.

Memories dance on a fragile thread,
Between the smiles and words left unsaid.
Each moment stitched with love's embrace,
A tapestry worn with time's grace.

Through shadows deep, and colors bright,
We find our way to the softest light.
Grief mingles gently with giggles' sound,
In the heart's fabric, forever bound.

So let us toast to the joy and pain,
For both are threads in this life's domain.
A tapestry rich, though frayed and worn,
With grief and giggles, our hearts are sworn.

When the Heart Dances with Pain

A heart in turmoil starts to sway,
In the grip of sorrow, it learns to play.
With every beat, a story unfolds,
Of love and loss, of dreams bought and sold.

The rhythm aches, yet somehow lifts,
In shadows where the spirit drifts.
Each tear a note in a haunting score,
When pain takes hold, we dance for more.

Embracing wounds that time won't mend,
A silent partner, yet a faithful friend.
Through vacant nights and hopeful dawns,
The heart keeps dancing, until it's drawn.

This dance of grief, with beauty lined,
We find our way, though echoes bind.
In every step, the heart will strain,
But joy can rise when the heart dances with pain.

An Ode to Fleeting Joy

Like morning dew that fades by noon,
Joy glimmers brightly, a fleeting tune.
In laughter's spark and sunlight's ray,
We cherish moments that slip away.

A child's giggle, a lover's glance,
Each joyous heartbeat, a fleeting dance.
Caught in the web of time's embrace,
We hold onto joy, though it leaves no trace.

A whisper soft, a dance of light,
In the depths of shadows, we chase the bright.
With every joy, a hint of pain,
Yet through it all, we strive again.

So here's to joy, though short it seems,
In every heartbeat, in every dream.
We drink it deep, let it fill our soul,
For fleeting joy makes us whole.

The Ephemeral Art of Sorrow

In twilight's brush, the sorrows blend,
A canvas painted, where heartaches mend.
Each stroke a tear, each shade a pain,
In the ephemeral art, we find our gain.

Like whispers of wind through the silent trees,
Sorrow drifts softly, carried by breeze.
Yet in that ache, a beauty thrives,
A paradox where the spirit survives.

We craft our grief in silent nights,
Transforming wounds into fragile lights.
An artist's heart, forever torn,
In this canvas of life, we are reborn.

So let us cherish this art we weave,
In every sorrow, we learn to believe.
For fleeting beauty, like shadows cast,
Is the ephemeral art that forever lasts.

The Comedy of Crying Souls

In shadows deep, the laughter stings,
While heavy hearts wear painted wings.
The jesters joke, in sorrow's play,
As tears of joy drip down the gray.

A masquerade of smiles and weeps,
Where sorrow thrives, the laughter creeps.
A dance of souls, both bright and dim,
In solemn jest, they sing on whim.

Behind the mask, a truth unfolds,
A tale of pain that fate beholds.
The craft of joy in sorrow's art,
Elastic smiles, a fragile heart.

So let us laugh in wistful pain,
In this grand play, we all remain.
Through every jest, through every tear,
A comedy sung for all to hear.

Crystalline Drops of Joyful Pain

Each drop a glint of bittersweet,
Reflecting joy in sorrow's seat.
Crystalline tears, they fall like rain,
A dance of joy wrapped in the pain.

A whisper soft, the heart does bend,
In twilight glow, where shadows blend.
The light breaks free from sorrow's clutch,
In precious drops, we feel the touch.

What joy resides in pain's embrace,
In each clear drop, a fleeting trace.
An echo of laughter mingled tight,
A bittersweet and soft delight.

So raise a glass to joy and woe,
In every drop, the truth we sow.
For through the pain, the soul can gain,
Crystalline drops of joyful pain.

Radiant Giggles Beneath the Clouds

The sun peeks out, a cheeky grin,
As giggles hide where storms begin.
Beneath the clouds, a lullaby,
The whispers danced along the sky.

In playful shades of gray and white,
The laughter twirls, a pure delight.
A symphony of sounds that play,
In gentle breezes, soft ballet.

Upon the ground, the shadows dance,
As nature sings a merry chance.
The raindrops laugh in joyful spree,
As earth and sky unite in glee.

So let the giggles fill your soul,
As clouds drift by, we feel the whole.
For in this world, where laughter's found,
Radiant giggles make life sound.

The Paradox of Grinning Sadness

Within the smile, a sorrow sighs,
In every laugh, a truth belies.
The heart does ache while lips may cheer,
A paradox that draws us near.

We wear the masks to hide the pain,
With grinning faces, we entertain.
In shadows cast, we play our part,
A sweet facade guards every heart.

Oh, how we laugh, with aching souls,
In vibrant tones, our spirit rolls.
Yet deep inside, the silence thorns,
A bittersweet that never mourns.

So let us cherish every tear,
The grinning sadness we hold dear.
For in this dance, our truths collide,
A paradox where love abides.

Glitter in the Gloom

In shadows deep where whispers play,
A spark of light begins to sway.
Through the dark, it weaves a dance,
Inviting hearts to take a chance.

The silence hums a secret tune,
As stars appear beneath the moon.
Each glimmer tells a tale unsung,
Of dreams reborn and love that's young.

Even when the night is cold,
The glitter shines, a sight to hold.
In every tear, a chance to see,
The beauty that can set us free.

So let your spirit find a way,
To turn the night into bright day.
For in the gloom, we'll find our flight,
With every spark, we chase the light.

The Sadness that Sparks Joy

In a tear, a memory glows,
A bittersweet that gently flows.
The heartache whispers, soft and light,
Yet holds a spark to burn so bright.

A shadow hides the tender dream,
Yet in the dark, there's hope, it seems.
With every heartbeat, life can show,
The hidden paths where joy can grow.

In moments wrapped in gentle sighs,
A laughter born from soft goodbyes.
For sadness wears a joyful cloak,
In every word that love once spoke.

So dance between the tears and cheer,
Embrace the joy that lives right here.
In every shadow, let it flow,
The sadness that sparks joy, we'll know.

A Melodic Hitchhike through Heartache

On empty roads, the echoes play,
A melody of night and day.
Each note a tear, each chord a sigh,
A hitchhike through the reasons why.

The freight trains hum a lonesome tune,
Beneath the silver, watch the moon.
With every mile, I find my way,
Through heartache's grip, I learn to stay.

With every stop, a tale unfolds,
Of broken dreams and courage bold.
The music wraps around my soul,
A gentle path to make me whole.

So ride along the beat of time,
In heartache's song, I find my rhyme.
For joy and pain blend in their art,
A hitchhike through the aching heart.

Shadows Singing Sweet Songs

Beneath the veil where whispers creep,
The shadows sing while lovers weep.
Their voices weave a haunting grace,
In every line, a soft embrace.

A lullaby of lost delight,
Echoes gently through the night.
In every sigh, a tale is spun,
Of battles lost and battles won.

Yet in their song, a hope still glows,
A promise hidden, sweetly flows.
For shadows sing of love so deep,
In every quiet heart, they seep.

So listen close, let them be heard,
In every heart, a whispered word.
The shadows sing, their voices strong,
A symphony where we belong.

Laughter Beneath the Weeping Willow

Underneath the willow tree,
Laughter dances in the breeze.
Whispers of the past they see,
Echoes carried with such ease.

Children play upon the ground,
Joyful voices all around.
In the shade, their dreams are found,
With the leaves, their hopes are bound.

Time flows gently, bittersweet,
Every moment, a heartbeat.
In this haven, life's retreat,
Where laughter and the sorrow meet.

As the sunlight starts to fade,
Stories linger, never trade.
In this space, memories laid,
Laughter under willow's shade.

The Balm of Bitter Blessings

In shadows cast by heavy hearts,
Bitter truths play subtle parts.
Yet in sorrow, beauty starts,
Finding light where sadness darts.

A tearful smile, a fleeting grace,
Each moment holds a tender trace.
Lessons learned, a warm embrace,
In the dark, we find our place.

Hope's soft whispers fill the night,
Turn the pain towards the light.
Bitter blessings take their flight,
Making weary spirits bright.

Through the storm, the soul can mend,
Bitter paths may lead to friends.
In the chaos, love transcends,
Balm for wounds that time defends.

Crystalline Drops of Delight

Morning dew on tender leaves,
Crystalline, the heart believes.
Every drop, a world receives,
In their glimmer, joy achieves.

Sunrise paints the day anew,
Colors bursting, bright and true.
Nature sings a vibrant hue,
In each moment, life renews.

Tiny wonders all around,
In their beauty, hope is found.
Crystalline drops, soft and sound,
In their presence, love is crowned.

Life's small moments bring delight,
In each spark, the day feels right.
Dancing shadows, pure and light,
Crystalline drops, dreams take flight.

A Comedic Veil Over Sorrow

Laughter breaks the silent gloom,
Comedic masks in every room.
Jests unfold, dispelling doom,
Life's absurd through laughter's bloom.

In the shadows, jokes take flight,
Turning darkness into light.
With each laugh, we stand and fight,
Turning wrongs eventually right.

Humor hides what's hard to face,
In its warmth, we find our place.
Veiling sorrow with its grace,
Life's a game we all embrace.

From the tears, a new dawn grows,
In our hearts, the laughter flows.
Comedic veil around our woes,
In this dance, true healing shows.

Raspberry Ripples of Remembrance

In a garden lush, where shadows play,
Raspberries blush under the sun's sway.
Each plucked jewel whispers tales untold,
Of laughter and love from days of old.

The sweet scent floats on soft summer air,
Memories linger, precious and rare.
Ripples of time in a fragile bowl,
Taste the moments that nourish the soul.

A hand reaches out to capture the taste,
In fleeting seconds, no time to waste.
The berry's embrace, a warmth we crave,
A glimpse of the past, a path we pave.

With every bite, a journey begins,
Through raspberry dreams, where love always wins.
Remember the ripples, let them intwine,
In the heart's orchard, where memories shine.

When Joy Bows to Grief

In the twilight, laughter starts to fade,
Echoes of joy in the silence laid.
When sunlight dims and shadows grow,
A tender heart learns how to let go.

Time weaves between the moments we share,
Sown with love, yet burdened with care.
When joy bows down to the weight of sorrow,
We find strength to face a new tomorrow.

Grief carves paths in the heart's quiet space,
Each tear a reminder of love's embrace.
Through the valleys where shadows may creep,
We harvest memories, buried deep.

For every smile that dances anew,
There's a whisper of grief, soft yet true.
In this dance of loss, we learn to weave,
A tapestry of hope, where we believe.

Smirking through the Mist

Misty murmurs wrap the dawn in gray,
Yet, a smirk breaks through, brightening the day.
Clouds may whisper secrets draped in disguise,
But always shines the truth in the skies.

With each step forward, the fog starts to clear,
Laughter escapes, simple and sincere.
In the mysterious haze, shadows will dance,
Life's jest unfolds, giving hope a chance.

Whispers of dreams flicker, wild and free,
Smirking at shadows that wish to decree.
Bold hearts embrace the veils that they find,
Fleeting moments, adventures entwined.

Through the mist, a path begins to appear,
Guided by laughter, we conquer our fear.
Even when veiled in a shroud of despair,
We smirk at the trials, knowing we care.

The Flavor of Fleeting Elation

A burst of flavor, sweet on the tongue,
Moments of joy, eternally young.
Elation dances like fire in the air,
Brief as a sigh, yet stronger than care.

With bright laughter shared over dim-lit skies,
The flavor of friendship never truly dies.
Each fleeting glimmer, a treasure to hold,
In the tapestry of life, both vibrant and bold.

The pulse of excitement wraps round the heart,
A fleeting embrace that can never depart.
In delicious moments, we find our way,
Savoring life, come what may.

Though time may wane and seasons may shift,
The flavor of elation, a timeless gift.
With each taste, we indulge in the thrill,
Cherishing the joy that time cannot kill.

Milton Keynes UK
Ingram Content Group UK Ltd.
UKHW030750121124
451094UK00013B/816